A-3 Skywarrior

in action

By Jim Sullivan

Color By Don Greer & Tom Tullis

Illustrated by Joe Sewell

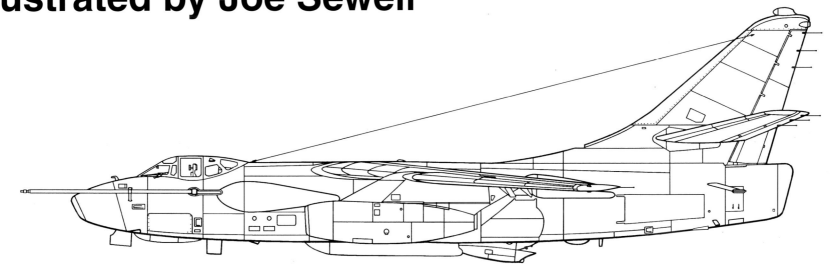

MW01011510

Aircraft Number 148

squadron/signal publications

An A3D-2/A3B (BuNo 142650) of VAH-5, The Savage Sons (of Sanford) thundered over the mountains of Southern France during its Mediterranean cruise while aboard USS Forrestal in the spring of 1962.

Dedication

This book is dedicated to the pilots, air crew and others who worked so hard to make the A-3 Skywarrior a success and who pioneered the way for the U.S. Navy's largest carrier based jet aircraft.

I would also like to dedicate this to my wife Linda and to Jim and Christy for being so patient and understanding for the many hours consumed while this book came together.

COPYRIGHT 1995 SQUADRON/SIGNAL PUBLICATIONS, INC.
1115 CROWLEY DRIVE CARROLLTON, TEXAS 75011-5010
All rights reserved. No part of this publication may be reproduced, stored in a retrieval system or transmitted in any form by means electrical, mechanical or otherwise, without written permission of the publisher.

ISBN 0-89747-328-0

If you have any photographs of aircraft, armor, soldiers or ships of any nation, particularly wartime snapshots, why not share them with us and help make Squadron/Signal's books all the more interesting and complete in the future. Any photograph sent to us will be copied and the original returned. The donor will be fully credited for any photos used. Please send them to:

Squadron/Signal Publications, Inc.
1115 Crowley Drive
Carrollton, TX 75011-5010

Acknowledgments

I would like to thank all the fine folks who provided information, stories, facts and photographs on the A-3 Skywarrior. In particular, I would like to acknowledge the extraordinary efforts put forth by Fred Carment and Bruce Trombecky to assist this author. My sincere thanks to all:

Al Adcock
LCDR W.D. Baldwin, USN (Ret.)
Roger Besecker
Bill Brabant
CAPT Fred Carment Jr.,USN (Ret.)
CAPT Jim de Ganahl, USN (Ret.)
Dr. Carlton Eddy
Thomas Gates
Harry Gann/McDonnell-Douglas
Joe Handelman, DDS
CAPT R.L. Huth, USN (Ret.)
Don Jay
Bob Lawson/The HOOK
Dave Lucabaugh
Ed Maloney
Jim Mesko
Doug Olson
Terry Panopalis
CAPT Herb L. Salyer, USN (Ret.)
William L. Swisher

Harold Andrews
Peter Bergagnini
Pete Bowers
Tom Chee
Tom Cuddy II
Robert F. Dorr
Bob Esposito
Fred Harl
LT Steve Halsted
Jan Jacobs
Clay Jansson
Duane Kasulka
Don Linn
Eric Lundahl
Peter Mersky
Rick Morgan
Lionel Paul
Bruce Trombecky
Don Spering/ A.I.R.
Charles E. Taylor

Carrying the modex "ZD" on the fin, this A3D-2 (BuNo 142236) of VAH-8, Det. L, was attached to Carrier Air Wing Twenty-one and flew from the USS MIDWAY during August of 1958. In November of 1962, this Skywarrior was lost in flight. (USN via Harold Andrews)

3

Introduction

Two major factors combined to bring about the development of the A-3 Skywarrior. The first was the advent of the jet engine and the second was the technology of nuclear weapons. With the development of the Atomic bomb and its tremendous destructive power, it was obvious to the military that nuclear weapons were here to stay. The Army Air Force had the Boeing B-29 Superfortress to deliver a nuclear pay load from land bases, and the U.S. Navy also wanted the capability to deliver such a load from its carrier based force. With the service introduction of the P2V-3C Neptune, the Navy acquired the capability they had sought, but with one severe limitation. The Lockheed Neptune could take off from a carrier deck with the help of JATO (Jet Assisted Take Off). This was demonstrated during March of 1949. The problem was that such a mission would be a one-way trip from the carrier, since the Neptune lacked the capability of landing back aboard and had to reach a land base. The P2V-3C did; however, provide a temporary answer to the nuclear delivery needs of the Navy.

In February of 1951, the North American AJ-I Savage was introduced to the fleet and became the first operational nuclear carrier based bomber. It was fully carrier qualified and could launch and recover from the decks of the carriers on a round-trip basis. The Savage was, at that time, the largest aircraft to be operationally assigned to the carriers and was quite a handful for the deck crews to manage. The AJ-1 was a prop-jet combination powered by two Pratt & Whitney 2,400 hp R-2800-48 radial engines and two 4,600 lbst Allison J-33A-10 turbojet engines, giving it a top speed of 450 mph. For the Navy's nuclear needs, the AJ-1 superseded the P2V-3C; however, the Navy wanted an all-jet attack bomber and the higher operational speeds that it could provide.

In the Navy's quest for such a bomber, no less than a dozen companies expressed an interest in bidding for the contract but, in the final analysis, it boiled down to Curtiss and Douglas, with Douglas presenting the best design (the model 593-8). Through the experienced guidance of Ed Heiniman, Douglas provided a lightweight but sturdy concept that was initially scoffed at by the Navy, who thought that a nuclear attack bomber should weigh considerably more. Heiniman proved them wrong and the first XA3D-1 (BuNo 125412) was completed and first flown from Edwards AFB on 28 October 1952.

As with any new aircraft, some design problems surfaced, but these were quickly resolved. In early flight testing it quickly became apparent that the 7,000 lbst Westinghouse J-40 turbojet engines were insufficient for the big Skywarrior. With the availability of the more powerful Pratt and Whitney J-57 turbojet engines, that problem was resolved. Some design changes were necessitated by this larger engine, including the installation of a larger engine nacelle and stronger engine pylon. Developing over 9,500 pounds of thrust at military power, the J-57 delivered sufficient power for the Skywarrior to meet its design intent. For a maximum load take-off or short field operation, twelve JATO bottles could be attached to provide extra thrust. These were installed on six attachment points located on both sides of the rear fuselage.

The prime design requirement for the Navy's largest jet was the capability to deliver a nuclear bomb load from the deck of an aircraft carrier. This concept was the Navy's answer to the USAF's Strategic Air Command (SAC). In keeping with its nuclear delivery capability, the Skywarrior airframe was developed around a five by five by fifteen foot bomb bay which was large enough to hold the rather bulky and heavy 10,000 pound nuclear bomb. That requirement necessitated the use of a high swept wing design, which proved to be ideal for the placement of the two engines. The installation of the resulting low-slung twin engine nacelles

The North American AJ-1 Savage was the first nuclear attack aircraft operationally assigned to operate round-trip from Navy carrier decks. It was powered by two piston and two jet engines that gave the aircraft a top speed of 450 mph. This AJ-1 (BuNo 124181) was assigned to NATC Patuxent River, Maryland during 1951. (Pete Bowers Collection)

The XA3D-1 (BuNo 125412) on the ramp at the Douglas factory in El Segundo, California during 1952. The prototype had tubular engine nacelles housing Westinghouse J-40 engines. All lettering was White on an overall Glossy Sea Blue finish while the forward portion of the engine nacelles was trimmed in Red. (Douglas via Bruce Trombecky)

The first, of two, prototype Skywarriors, XA3D-1 (BuNo 125412) in flight on 15 December 1952, during early factory flight testing had Westinghouse J-40 engines installed. These were soon replaced with the more powerful Pratt and Whitney J-57 turbojet engine. This airframe continued in various flight test programs until its retirement during mid-1956. (USN via Robert F. Dorr)

made access to the engines for maintenance much easier. The XA3D-1 had a pressurized cockpit crewed by three including the pilot with a single set of controls, a bombardier seated to the right of the pilot and a navigator, who was seated back-to-back with the pilot. The only defensive armament carried by the Skywarrior was a tail-mounted, remotely controlled pair of 20mm cannons with 500 rounds per gun. For compact storage aboard the carriers, the outer wing panels and vertical fin were hydraulically folded. The high wing was swept back thirty-six degrees and incorporated leading edge slats outboard of the engine nacelles. These slats operated automatically by aerodynamic loads and provided extra lift for the wing. During its production life, only two basic versions were built, the A3D-1 and A3D-2. Douglas produced fifty of the A3D-1 variant and 230 of the more powerful A3D-2s. As time and technology progressed, the Navy added more nuclear-capable aircraft to the fleet and the A-3 was pressed into other roles. It was modified for reconnaissance, electronic surveillance, trainer, tanker and VIP transport. A few airframes were also modified to serve as test beds for various mis-

sile and weapons systems and, as of this writing, are still flying in that capacity with private companies.

The original design for the Skywarrior had no provisions for ejection seats and even though the concept was seriously considered, none were ever fitted to the Navy's A-3s. Emergency escape was accomplished via an "escape chute" located on the bottom of the fuselage to the rear of the nose wheel compartment. The name "WHALE" was soon adopted for the A-3 because of its large size. On occasion, when coming over the carrier's fantail, it was called the "Aluminum Overcast", since its huge shadow blocked out the sun as it passed overhead. The performance of the XA3D-1 Skywarrior was noted by the USAF who immediately expressed an interest in the design for use as an attack bomber. USAF modifications were implemented and the result was a look-alike cousin that was designated as the B-66 Destroyer. Quite similar in external appearance to the Skywarrior, the B-66 was powered by a pair of 10,000 lbst Allison J71 turbojet engines. Even though the A-3 was the original airframe, the B-66 was produced in larger quantities than the Skywarrior, with a total of 294 Destroyers being manufactured against a total of 282 A-3s. The long service life of the A-3s continued until the last one was retired in 1991, a period of thirty-nine years, compared to the retirement of the B-66 which occurred in 1974. Indeed the A-3 Skywarrior was a remarkable aircraft with a proud history of service with the U.S. Navy.

Development

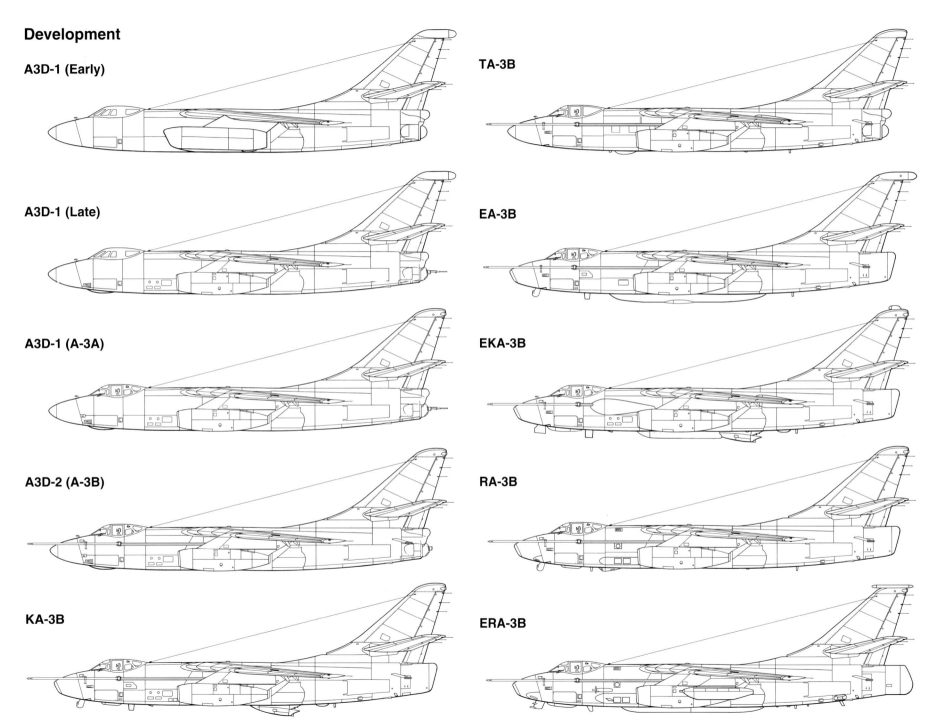

A3D-1 (Early)

A3D-1 (Late)

A3D-1 (A-3A)

A3D-2 (A-3B)

KA-3B

TA-3B

EA-3B

EKA-3B

RA-3B

ERA-3B

A3D-1/A-3A Skywarrior

Between 1953 and 1954, Douglas produced fifty of the first production model, the A3D-1 Skywarrior. Sleek and well ahead of its time, the production model differed little from the two prototypes, but were improved in the following areas: upgraded J-57 engines, the deletion of the fin tip fairing, redesigned and enlarged engine nacelles, redesigned canopy framing for better visibility, improved windshield wipers, improvements to the bomb bay to allow the aircraft to carry conventional as well nuclear bombs and provisions to carry mines or other special purpose ordnance. The first flight of a production A3D-1 took place at Los Angeles International Airport on 16 September 1953.

The tail-mounted Aero 21B twin 20MM cannon installation was retained in these early production models but was considered by many to be unnecessary and was systematically removed from most A3D-1 Skywarriors in favor of a new streamlined "dove tail" fairing containing defensive Electronic Counter Measures (ECM) equipment. The A3D-1 was powered by a pair of dependable 10,000 lbst Pratt & Whitney J-57 turbojet engines that gave the Skywarrior a top speed of 540 knots and a cruising speed of 460 knots. Although the A3D-1 could reach Mach One in a thirty degree dive, this speed range was avoided as control was next to impossible, since compressibility made the control surfaces very unresponsive.

To supplement take off power, the Skywarrior could utilize the boosting power of twelve JATO bottles which were attached to both sides of the rear fuselage with six attachment points

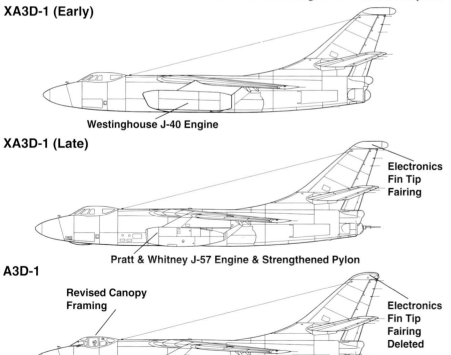

XA3D-1 (Early)

Westinghouse J-40 Engine

XA3D-1 (Late)

Electronics Fin Tip Fairing

Pratt & Whitney J-57 Engine & Strengthened Pylon

A3D-1

Revised Canopy Framing

Electronics Fin Tip Fairing Deleted

A3D-1 Skywarriors on the final assembly line at the Douglas El Segundo factory during 1955. These very early production A3D-1s had the fin cap antenna fairing. The aircraft in the background are AD-5W Skyraiders. (Douglas via Harry Gann)

Flying from the Naval Air Test Center (NATC) Patuxent River, Maryland during 1956, this Service Test A3D-1 (BuNo 135431) had its tail-mounted 20MM cannon removed. It continued to fly for the Navy for twelve years before being retired. The overall Glossy Sea Blue finish was retired in 1957, when the Navy changed to Gull Gray uppersurfaces over White undersurfaces. (USN via Fred Carment)

being located on the port and starboard sides. This JATO installation allowed the thirty-five ton "Whale" to take off in just four seconds, using less than the distance of a football field.

The Skywarrior performed many varied missions, but its primary purpose was that of a nuclear attack bomber. Other assignments were: conventional high altitude bomber, low level attack and pathfinder navigational escort for other Navy aircraft. On some occasions, the big Douglas jet was utilized as a high-speed jet airmail vehicle between ship and shore.

Crewed by three, the Skywarrior had a combat radius in excess of 1,000 nautical miles and a service ceiling of 40,000 feet. The bomb bay was capable of carrying a total of 8,700 pounds of bombs (nuclear or conventional) as well as mines and other special ordnance.

The first A3D-1 Skywarriors were assigned and delivered to VAH-1 at NAS Jacksonville, Florida during March of 1956. The modex used on that squadron's aircraft was "TB" which was used to acknowledge the commander of the unit, the well known and respected Second World War commander of the first Navy F4U Corsair combat squadron, VF-17, Captain Tommy Blackburn. The first operational assignment of the A3D-1 was in late 1956 aboard the USS FORRESTAL.

Although not factory installed on Skywarriors in the production line, A3D-1s were soon retrofitted with twenty-four foot deceleration/drag parachutes to help reduce the roll-out distance on land bases. The thirty-six degree swept back wing had leading edge slats outboard of the engine nacelles which were automatically actuated by aerodynamic loads and improved the lifting efficiency of the wing. In addition to the standard A3D-1 bomber configuration, Douglas converted one of the airframes (BuNo 130358), of the first production batch of fifty aircraft, to a photographic reconnaissance variant which was designated as the A3D-1P/RA-3A. This modification was accomplished by installing a photographic kit in the bomb bay, rendering it incapable of functioning as a bomber. Since it could no longer carry out its primary function, the aircraft was given the new designation A3D-1P. In addition to the photographic kit, camera ports were installed on each side of the fuselage, low and just forward of the bomb bay. Carrying as many as twelve cameras, the A3D-1P had provisions for dropping photo flash bombs or cartridges for night photographic missions.

Positioned on the port catapult of USS FORRESTAL, an A3D-1 (BuNo 135408) turns up as another A3D-1 (BuNo 135411) prepares to launch during carrier suitability trials. The trials were flown by Flight Test Skywarriors from NATC, Patuxent River, Maryland on 4 April 1956. (USN via Harold Andrews)

An A3D-1 comes over the ramp aboard USS FORRESTAL during the carrier suitability trials on 4 April 1956. The A3D was sometimes referred to as the "Aluminum Overcast" because it was the largest aircraft aboard the carrier. (Douglas via Jim Mesko)

The Skywarrior had hydraulic folding outer wing panels and a folding vertical fin. These aircraft are assigned to the NATC for flight test and evaluation and both have the 20MM cannon turret installed. (Douglas via Jim Mesko)

This A3D-1 is being positioned on the deck edge elevator for a trip down to the hangar deck aboard USS FORRESTAL on 5 April 1956. This A3D-1 Skywarrior was the thirteenth aircraft off the production line. (USN via Jim Mesko)

A Flight Test A3D-1 moves toward the forward deck edge elevator aboard USS FORRE-STAL during the aircraft's carrier suitability trials. To fit on the hangar deck, the wings and fin had to be folded. (USN via Harry Andrews)

The only other variation of the original batch of fifty A3D-1s was the electronic reconnais-sance version, the A3D-1Q/EA-3A. Five airframes were converted by Douglas (BuNo 130356 and BuNos 130360-130363). These aircraft carried a crew of seven, four ECM opera-tors and the standard flight crew of three. The A3D-1Q was first flown in May of 1955.

The ECM operators were responsible for gathering electronic intelligence information on enemy emitter sites. The A3D-1Q version carried ECM antennas in two fuselage blisters located just to the rear and under the cockpit. A small ECM ventral "canoe" was added to the forward underside of the fuselage. Those features made it easy to identify the A3D-1Q, some-times referred to as the "Queer Whale" because of its external differences with the standard A3D-1 configuration.

As the next variant, the A3D-2/A-3B entered production, starting in 1956, the A3D-1s faded away quickly and were relegated to training assignments, special use missions or retired. The A3D-1 Skywarrior was the Navy's first all-jet nuclear attack bomber and largest aircraft to be assigned to operational carrier deployment. As the long service career of the A-3 unfolded, many more uses and designations would follow.

(Right) Flying over the water off the southern coast of Maryland during December of 1956 this A3D-1 (BuNo 135431) was fitted with the more powerful P&W J-57 turbojet engines. The aircraft was assigned to NATC and flew with the Navy until early 1966 when it was retired. (USN via Harold Andrews)

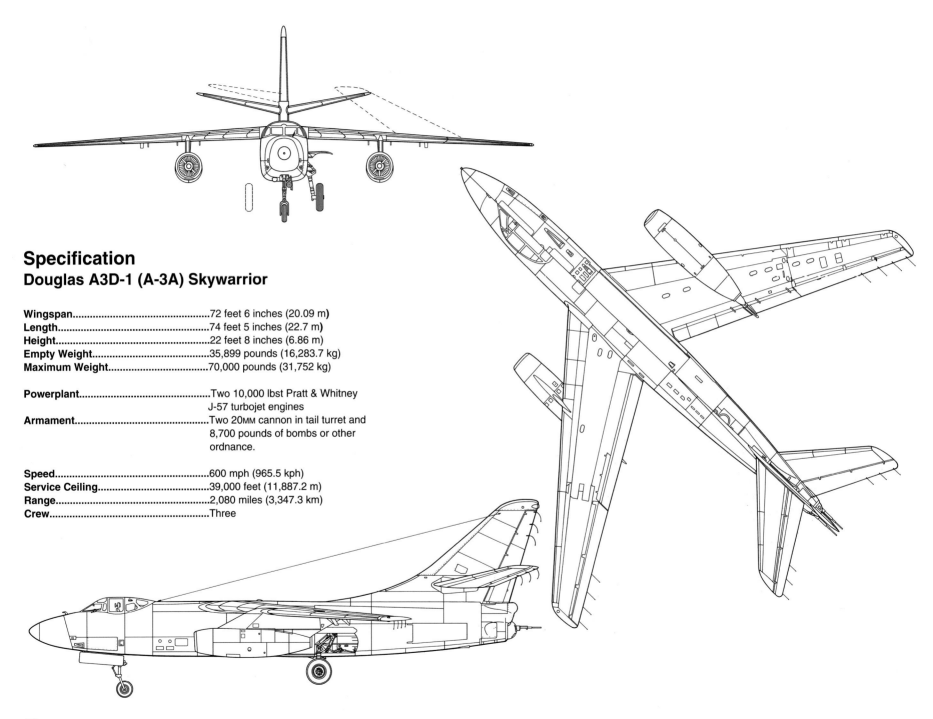

Specification
Douglas A3D-1 (A-3A) Skywarrior

Wingspan	72 feet 6 inches (20.09 m)
Length	74 feet 5 inches (22.7 m)
Height	22 feet 8 inches (6.86 m)
Empty Weight	35,899 pounds (16,283.7 kg)
Maximum Weight	70,000 pounds (31,752 kg)
Powerplant	Two 10,000 lbst Pratt & Whitney J-57 turbojet engines
Armament	Two 20mm cannon in tail turret and 8,700 pounds of bombs or other ordnance.
Speed	600 mph (965.5 kph)
Service Ceiling	39,000 feet (11,887.2 m)
Range	2,080 miles (3,347.3 km)
Crew	Three

An overall Glossy Sea Blue Heavy Two (VAH-2), Royal Rampants, A3D-1 Skywarrior parked on the ramp with its wings and tail folded during 1956. The aircraft still had the 20MM tail-mounted cannon in place. All lettering was in White and the nose radome was left unpainted. (Pete Bowers)

An A3D-1 (BuNo 135440) just off the Douglas El Segundo assembly line on 14 April 1956 painted in the Navy Gloss Gull Gray over White paint scheme. This Skywarrior was later assigned to Tommy Blackburn's VAH-1 and was lost in flight during August of 1959. (Douglas via Robert F. Dorr)

(Above and below) Douglas produced a close cousin to the Navy Skywarrior for the USAF under the designation B-66 Destroyer. There were 294 Destroyers manufactured and externally they strongly resembled the big Navy jet. The B-66 served several roles with the Air Force from 1953 to 1974 when they were retired. (Peter Bowers Collection)

This A3D-1 (BuNo 130356) had JATO rockets installed on the fuselage stations and still had the twin 20MM tail cannon installed. The aircraft was on display during the Dayton, Ohio airshow on 7 October 1954. The aircraft also carried the early production fin mounted electronics antenna fairing. (Gordy via Pete Bowers)

Sitting side-by-side in front of the Operations building at NAS Glenview in September of 1955, the number four production A3D-1 (BuNo 130355) differed little from the XA3D-1 prototype (BuNo 125412). Douglas produced a total of fifty A3D-1 Skywarriors. (Eric Lundahl via Clay Jansson)

Activated in late 1955 at NAS Jacksonville, Florida, VAH-1 Skywarriors were delivered in Glossy Sea Blue. Heavy One first deployed aboard ship in October of 1956 embarking in USS FORRESTAL. (USN via Pete Bowers)

This A3D-1 (BuNo 135438) of VAH-1 used twelve JATO bottles to dramatically shorten its take off run from NAS Jacksonville during 1957. With JATO assistance, the thirty-five ton bomber could lift off in four seconds in less than the length of a football field. (USN via Harold Andrews)

An A3D-1 (BuNo 135436) of VAH-1 lets down just over the fantail of USS FORRE-STAL on 26 June 1957. Heavy One flew the A3D Skywarrior until late 1962 when it retired its last Whale and transitioned to the North American A-5 Vigilante. (Douglas via Harold Andrews)

Marked with a Dayglow Orange vertical fin, this A-3A (BuNo 135435) was being refueled at the Naval Air Test Facility, Lakehurst, New Jersey during 1964. A3D-1s were redesignated as A-3As during August of 1962. This aircraft has the tail guns replaced with ECM equipment. The chevron on the fin was Dayglow Orange bordered by Black and White stripes. (Clay Jansson)

This cannon-armed A3D-1 (BuNo 135413) had its bomb bay doors open while on the ramp at the Naval Air Special Weapons Facility in Albuquerque, New Mexico during 1958. In the Fall of 1963, this Skywarrior was lost in flight. (Pete Bowers)

A flight of three A3D-1 Skywarriors (BuNos 142242, 138955 and 138906) of VAH-13 jettison fuel in flight over the Pacific near San Diego, California on 29 November 1961. A fuel dump vent was located on the bottom of each wing for fast dumping of aviation fuel in order to get the aircraft down to landing weight quickly. (USN via Harold Andrews)

Flying high near snow-capped Mt. Fuji in Japan, an A3D-1 of VAH-2 begins its turn for a landing heading to NAS Atsugi during late 1957. Part of Carrier Air Group Five aboard the USS BON HOMME RICHARD, Heavy Two was home-based at NAS Whidbey Island, Washington. (USN via Herb Salyer)

Tail Turret

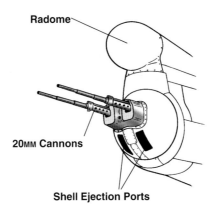
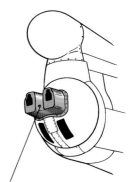

Radome

20MM Cannons

Shell Ejection Ports

20MM Cannons Deleted

An A-3A of VAH-123, the West coast RAG (Replacement Air Group) squadron, on final approach for NAS Whidbey Island, Washington. The RAG trained pilots and other air crew for Fleet assignment with the Skywarrior from 1959 until 1971. (USN via Harold Andrews)

This A-3A (BuNo 135435) was as compact as it could get while parked on the ramp at the Naval Electronics Laboratory on 16 October 1968. A uniquely shaped speed brake on the fuselage bottom is located just to the rear of the open entry/escape chute. (Roger Besecker)

This A3D-1Q (BuNo 130363) was the last of a batch of five standard bombers converted to the electronic reconnaissance role. This Skywarrior, parked on the ramp at the Naval Missile Center, Point Mugu, California on 19 May 1962, carried a crew of seven, adding four ECM operators to the standard flight crew. The tear drop shaped fuselage blister below and to the rear of the cockpit helped identify the A3D-1Q. (Doug Olson via Clay Jansson)

After serving proudly in VAH-3, this A-3A Skywarrior (BuNo 135423) was relegated to the bone yard at Davis Monthan AFB on 21 March 1966. It was later brought back to flying status and assigned for ground training work at NAS Alameda, California. The Heavy Three Sea Dragon unit insignia was carried on the forward fuselage just to the rear of the cockpit. (Clay Jansson)

This A3D-1 (BuNo 135413) of the U.S. Naval Air Special Weapons Facility, made a wheels-up landing at Kirtland AFB, New Mexico on 3 September 1956. The Whale was soon repaired and served with the Fleet until September of 1963 when it was destroyed in a crash. (U.S. Navy)

This A3D-1Q (BuNo 130361) was the third airframe converted to the electronic reconnaissance role. The Skywarrior was on loan to Westinghouse and the Army for testing their SLAR (Side Looking Airborne Radar) pod (similar to the one later installed on the OV-I Mohawk) during 1966. (Dave Lucabaugh Collection)

15

A3D-2/A-3B Skywarrior

The A3D-2/A-3B Skywarrior airframe was the final and definitive version produced by Douglas. The company built 164 A3D-2s, thirty A3D-2P/RA-3Bs, twenty-four A3D-2Q/EA-3Bs and twelve A3D-2T/TA-3Bs. All other variants were modifications/conversions by Douglas and/or the Navy. The A3D-2 first flew on 12 June 1956 and featured a number of improvements over the earlier A3D-1. These improvements included the installation of the more powerful 10,500 lbst Pratt and Whitney J-57-P-10 turbojet engines. These engines gave the A3D-2 a combat radius of 1,200 miles and a top speed of 558 knots. The bomb bay was modified to carry 12,800 pounds of nuclear or conventional bombs, as well as mines or other special purpose ordnance. The aircraft was also modified with a refueling probe mounted on the port fuselage side. The addition of the inflight refueling capability greatly expanded the operating range of the A3D-2 and with the later addition of a tanker package, the Skywarrior was given a prolonged service life that lasted into the early 1990's. Other improvements included reliable anti-skid brakes, pressurized crew cockpit and forward portion of the bomb bay compartment and a heavier, stronger canopy.

Although some early A3D-2s had the twin 20MM tail stinger installed on the production line, most were quickly removed in favor of the "dove tail" streamlined fairing and the defensive ECM systems it housed. The A3D-2 also saw the first use of the "flat" nose radome that housed an AN/ASB-7 radar. This same type of flat nosed radome was retrofitted on many earlier A3D-1s that were still in service. The A3D-2 had a gross weight of 70,000 pounds.

The first batch of A3D-2s began to reach the fleet early in 1957 and were assigned to VAH-2. Douglas continued to produce A3D-2 Skywarriors over a three year period with the final one being completed early in 1960. A grand total of 230 airframes were completed. Like its predecessor, the A3D-2 had folding outer wing panels and a folding vertical tail, all hydraulically operated, as were the extendible fuselage speed brake. Although from the start the swept wing design had automatically actuated slats outboard of the engine nacelles, an improvement was introduced with the cambered leading edge wing, which extended the slats from the inner side of the engine nacelles to the fuselage, which greatly improved the handling of the Skywarrior on take off and landing.

The twenty-four foot deceleration/drag parachute installation was included for use on short-er airfields at smaller land bases. One former Whale-driver volunteered the following story. One very cold winter day, his A-3 was to ferry some Naval types from the boat to two different land bases. All went well from take off and everything progressed normally including touchdown at the first base where the drag chute was deployed and functioned as advertised. As the Skywarrior slowed down on the rainy, cold runway, the pilot turned off the duty runway onto the taxiway and proceeded to the operations building to discharge his passenger. The wet parachute was hurriedly repacked and stowed in its compartment and the A-3 departed for the second Naval Air Station. After a short uneventful flight, the A-3 lined up for the duty runway and immediately after a perfect touchdown deployed the drag chute. To everyone's amazement, a perfectly formed orange ice cube came tumbling out of the rear compartment and hopped along behind the A-3 for the length of the runway. With no actual damage done and with more than a few snickers, the A-3 discharged its passenger and departed post-haste. Coincidentally, a squadron memo was later issued to carry a spare, dry chute for such encounters.

Another story related to the exploits of the Whale was submitted by a former pilot who shall remain anonymous. He related the following narrow escape, it seems that during a hasty departure from the flight deck, this pilot forgot to lower his flaps during a day launch. No one, including himself, caught the oversight and the A-3 was positioned for the catapult shot and given the signal to launch. The pilot returned the salute and braced. The steam cat did its job and as the Skywarrior accelerated down the deck, everything appeared normal. As the Whale became airborne, the pilot realized he did not have the usual lift and immediately discovered that he had not lowered his flaps for take off. He engaged them instantly as the A-3 began to settle toward the water. As the flaps caught hold and began to provide some additional lift, he skimmed the water in a three-point attitude for what must have been the longest ten seconds in the world. Slowly, but surely, the A-3 began to climb and thankfully, Davey Jones did not claim the Whale that day (shades of Jimmy Doolittle's B-25 take off from the USS HORNET on the Tokyo raid).

Many of the A3D-2/A-3B Skywarriors were modified from their original designations and served in one or more additional roles before their service lives were completed. A-3s served the U.S. Navy up to and including the Gulf War in 1990. Quite an admirable record for an airframe conceived in the late 1940's. Douglas had valid reason for their pride in producing the venerable A-3 Skywarrior.

Decorated with a sharks mouth, this overall Glossy Sea Blue Skywarrior was the first off the production line (eventually 164 airframes) to carry the designation A3D-2. After the DOD changed the designation system in August of 1962, the A3D-2 became the A-3B. Although the A3D-2 had no prototype, this Skywarrior (BuNo 138902) had test instrumentation installed in the nose. A small Douglas emblem was positioned just to the rear of the white '902' on the nose. (Ed Maloney via Clay Jansson)

Radome Development

A3D-1/A-3A

Pointed Radome

A3D-2/A-3B

"Flat Nosed" Radome

(Right) This A3D-2 (BuNo 142247) of VAH-6, Carrier Air Group Nine (CVG-9) aboard USS RANGER was spotted (parked) on the deck edge elevator during 1961. The aircraft retained its twin 20MM tail cannon and was painted in the standard Gloss Gull Gray over White scheme with all lettering in Black. (Bruce Trombecky Collection)

All down and dirty, this A3D-2 of VAH-5 was just seconds away from trapping aboard the USS FORRESTAL during the ship's Mediterranean cruise in February of 1962. Pilots always tried to catch the number three arresting wire, which was considered a perfect landing. (USN via Fred Carment)

An A3D-2 (BuNo 138921) of VAH-3 deployed its twenty-four foot deceleration/drag chute on landing at NAS Sanford, Florida during 1961. This drag chute reduced the landing rollout and was used exclusively when operating from land bases. (USN via Peter Mersky)

This A3D-2 (BuNo 138905) was the fourth Skywarrior off the A3D-2 production line. It was soon redesignated as a YA3D-2 and assigned to Service Test at the Naval Air Test Center, Patuxent River, Maryland, to test stability and engine performance. The aircraft was visiting NAS Anacostia, on 25 October 1958. (Dave Lucabaugh)

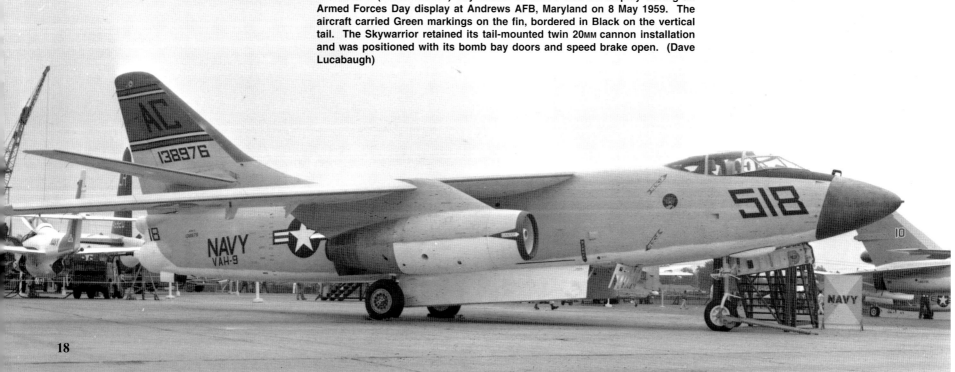

This A3D-2 (BuNo 138976) Skywarrior of VAH-9 was on display during an Armed Forces Day display at Andrews AFB, Maryland on 8 May 1959. The aircraft carried Green markings on the fin, bordered in Black on the vertical tail. The Skywarrior retained its tail-mounted twin 20MM cannon installation and was positioned with its bomb bay doors and speed brake open. (Dave Lucabaugh)

This A3D-2 (BuNo 142659) of VAH-5 Savage Sons (based at NAS Sanford) was spotted just forward of the island during a gunnery exercise aboard USS FORRESTAL in the Spring of 1962. The aircraft's folding wings saved precious deck space. (USN via Fred Carment)

Bringing a twenty-five ton bomber aboard a carrier made for some exciting moments. This A3D-2 (BuNo 142661) of Heavy Five snagged the wire and came to a halt after it dipped its port wingtip while recovering aboard USS FORRESTAL in February of 1962. (USN via Fred Carment)

Tail Cone Development

A3D-1 (A-3A)

Aero 20mm Gun Turret

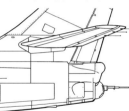

A3D-2 (A-3B)

Aero 20mm Gun Turret With Guns Replaced With DECM

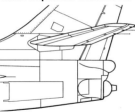

A3D-2 (A-3B)

DECM "Dove Tail" Installation

This A3D-2 (142630) of VAH-5 made a perfect landing during routine flight operations aboard the USS FORRESTAL during early 1962. Skywarriors 608 and 609 carry the Battle Efficiency "E" marking on the fuselage beneath the cockpit on a White shield. (USN via Fred Carment)

An A3D-2 (135434) of VAH-3 pours on the power for another pass after taking a wave off from the LSO during carrier flight operations in 1959. This Skywarrior served the Fleet until mid-1967 when it was retired. The airframe was later destroyed intentionally as a practice tool for fire fighting training. (Clay Jansson)

19

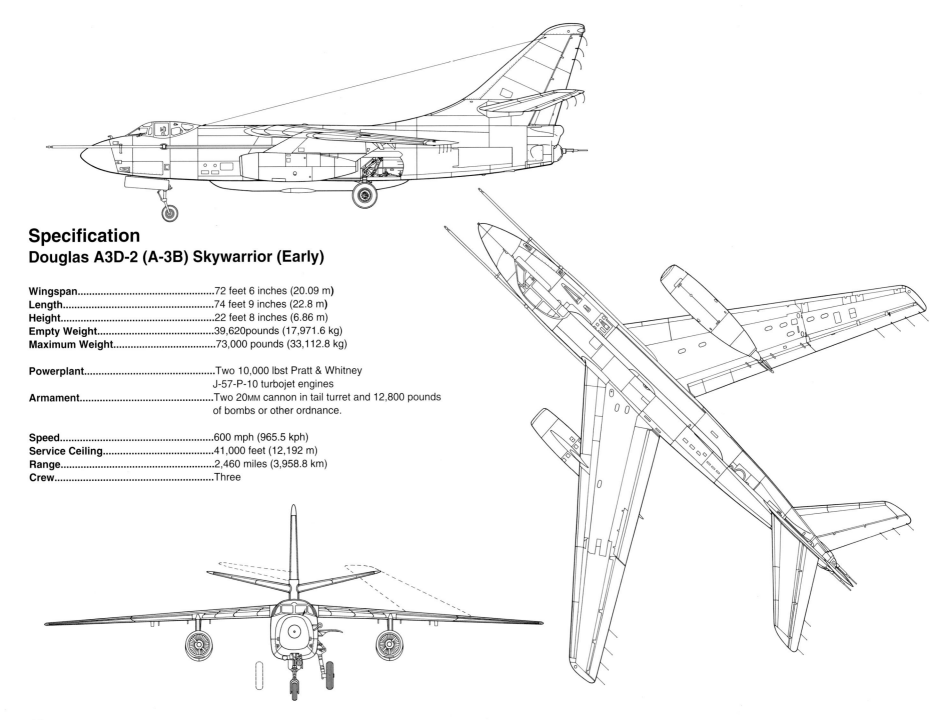

Specification
Douglas A3D-2 (A-3B) Skywarrior (Early)

Wingspan...72 feet 6 inches (20.09 m**)**
Length...74 feet 9 inches (22.8 m**)**
Height...22 feet 8 inches (6.86 m)
Empty Weight...39,620pounds (17,971.6 kg)
Maximum Weight.....................................73,000 pounds (33,112.8 kg)

Powerplant...Two 10,000 lbst Pratt & Whitney
J-57-P-10 turbojet engines
Armament...Two 20ᴍᴍ cannon in tail turret and 12,800 pounds
of bombs or other ordnance.

Speed...600 mph (965.5 kph)
Service Ceiling.......................................41,000 feet (12,192 m)
Range...2,460 miles (3,958.8 km)
Crew...Three

Seven White stars on a Red band and Red tail stripes identify this A3D-2 (BuNo 142664) visiting MCAS Yuma, on 12 March 1959, as being assigned to VAH-7. The open door on the bottom aft fuselage beneath the tail is the drag chute compartment. This aircraft has had the 20MM cannon armament removed. (Clay Jansson)

This A3D-2 (BuNo 138976) of VAH-11, parked on the ramp at MCAS Yuma, on 12 March 1959, carried a Black checkerboard design on the tip of the vertical fin. Heavy Eleven was attached to Carrier Air Group One, aboard USS FRANKLIN D. ROOSEVELT. (Clay Jansson)

21

This A-3B (BuNo 138947) of VAH-10 came to a halt after engaging the barrier aboard the USS CONSTELLATION ON 6 August 1962. This Skywarrior suffered minimum damage and was quickly returned to flying status. Unfortunately, it was lost three years later during an operational accident in Tonkin Gulf. (USN via Peter Mersky)

Highly modified and redesignated as a NA-3B, this Skywarrior (BuNo 142256) was bailed to Westinghouse for research work tracking re-entry vehicles during February of 1964. Special optical equipment was installed in the made-to-fit B-50 turret located just behind the cockpit. (Bruce Trombecky Collection)

This A-3B (BuNo 142401) of VAH-13 served with Carrier Air Group Eleven aboard USS KITTY HAWK (CVA-63). The unit was based at NAS Whidbey Island, Washington when not deployed. (Doug Olson via Clay Jansson)

(Left) These A-3B's of VAH-2 carried the "NL" modex in Black and were part of Carrier Air Group Fifteen aboard the USS CORAL SEA during late 1962. All three Skywarriors had the dove-tail tail cone fairing replacing the original 20MM gun turret. (USN via Peter Mersky)

This A-3B (BuNo 138922) of VAQ-33 had a replacement starboard speed brake from another aircraft, giving it two fuselage national insignias for a brief period during September of 1974. The FEWSG legend on the fuselage stands for Fleet Electronic Warfare Support Group. (Don Spering/ A.I.R. Collection)

Based at NAS Whidbey Island, Washington, this A-3B (BuNo 144627), visiting NAS North Island, California during 1967, served with VAH-4. During the Vietnam war, Heavy Four detachments served on no less than seven different carriers. (William L. Swisher via Dave Lucabaugh)

Assigned to Carrier Air Group Eleven, this A3D-2 (BuNo 142401) of VAH-13 parked on the ramp at NAS North Island, California on 25 August 1962, carried the "GP" modex on the fin. This Skywarrior was later reconfigured as a KA-3B and flew tanker missions during the war in Vietnam. (Clay Jansson)

An A-3B (142632) of VAH-10 on the transit ramp at NAS North Island, California on 2 May 1964. VAH-10 was attached to Carrier Air Wing Fourteen aboard the USS CONSTELLATION. The aircraft carried ten White Stars on a Red field on the fin tip. (Clay Jansson)

Dumping fuel from its underwing vents to get down to proper landing weight, this A3D-2 (BuNo 138933) of VAH-1 is preparing to land aboard USS INDEPENDENCE. This Skywarrior was assigned to Carrier Air Group Seven during 1961. (USN via Harold Andrews)

An A-3B (BuNo 144628) of VAQ-130 spotted on the ramp at NATC Patuxent River, Maryland on 23 April 1973. After service in the Vietnam war, Tactical Electronic Warfare Squadron One Thirty was assigned the job of training A-3 crews on the East coast. (Jim Sullivan)

This A-3B (BuNo 142652) of VAH-4 had the tanker package installed in the bomb bay for aerial refueling duties. The Skywarrior had just recovered aboard the USS KITTY HAWK which was operating in the Tonkin Gulf off Vietnam during 1965. (Lionel Paul)

23

An A-3B (BuNo 142664) of VAH-11 in formation with a pair of F-4B Phantoms (BuNos 149419 & 149431) of VF-14 on 4 May 1964. Both squadrons were attached to Carrier Air Group One aboard the USS FRANKLIN D. ROOSEVELT (CVA-42). This Skywarrior had the tanker package installed in the bomb bay for aerial refueling. (USN via Peter Mersky)

Returning from a strike over North Vietnam, an A-3B (BuNo 142255) of VAH-4 was escorted by a F-8J (BuNo 149139) of VF-51. Both aircraft were attached to Carrier Air Group Five aboard the USS TICONDEROGA during 1962. (USN via Peter Mersky)

Refueling Package

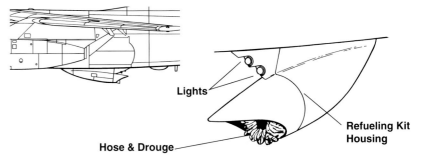

Lights

Refueling Kit Housing

Hose & Drouge

Refueling Capability

After trying several systems, Douglas perfected a reel and hose refueling system and introduced the tanker package to the fleet. The package allowed the standard A3D-2/A-3B to inflight refuel other aircraft, a capability much appreciated by aircraft low on fuel. This tanker-package could be installed or removed in three to four hours, allowing the Skywarrior to serve as an aerial tanker or as a bomber. The addition of the tanker-package did not affect the designation of the Skywarrior, it remained A3D-2/A-3B. When the permanent inflight refueling system was installed on Whales early in 1967, the designation of the dedicated tanker was changed to KA-3B

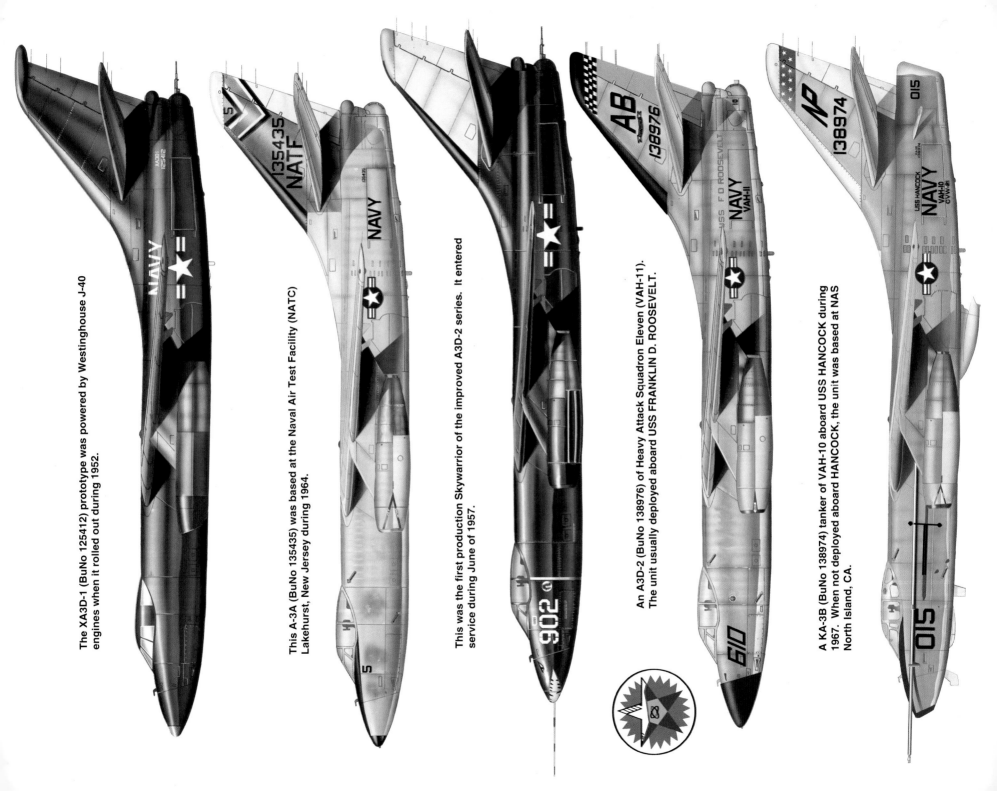

The XA3D-1 (BuNo 125412) prototype was powered by Westinghouse J-40 engines when it rolled out during 1952.

This A-3A (BuNo 135435) was based at the Naval Air Test Facility (NATC) Lakehurst, New Jersey during 1964.

This was the first production Skywarrior of the improved A3D-2 series. It entered service during June of 1957.

An A3D-2 (BuNo 138976) of Heavy Attack Squadron Eleven (VAH-11). The unit usually deployed aboard USS FRANKLIN D. ROOSEVELT.

A KA-3B (BuNo 138974) tanker of VAH-10 aboard USS HANCOCK during 1967. When not deployed aboard HANCOCK, the unit was based at NAS North Island, CA.

This EKA-3B (BuNo 124452) of VAQ-131 served aboard USS JOHN F. KENNEDY during August of 1970.

VAQ-131

A TA-3B trainer (BuNo 144861) of RVAH-3 at NAS Sanford, FL during May of 1967.

RVAH-3

This RA-3B (BuNo 144840) of VAP-61 was stationed at NAS North Island, CA during 1968 between deployments to Vietnam.

An ERA-3B (BuNo 144846) electronic warfare aircraft of VAQ-34 stationed at Point Mugu, CA during June of 1985. These aircraft often served as electronic threat simulators during fleet exercises.

An EA-3B of Fleet Reconnaissance Squadron One (VQ-1) aboard USS RANGER during November of 1976.

This KA-3B (BuNo 138974) was a dedicated tanker and served with VAH-10 aboard the USS HANCOCK as a part of Carrier Air Wing Twenty-One. With all bombing equipment removed, this Skywarrior had a single role mission, aerial tanker. The aircraft was visiting NAS North Island, California on 28 April 1967. (Clay Jansson)

KA-3B

Although as early as 1959, A3D-2/A-3B Skywarriors had the capability to conduct aerial refueling via the tanker-package, it was felt that it was necessary to expand this capability as the war in Vietnam intensified and the dedicated tanker variant of the A-3 evolved. Over the course of the war in Southeast. Asia, some 400 battle-damaged aircraft or those low on fuel were "saved" by tanker Whales.

The conversion of the A3D-2/A-3B airframes was handled by NARF (Naval Air Rework Facility) Alameda, California, who, by the end of 1968, had converted eighty-five A3D-2/A-3B attack bombers to the KA-3B tanker configuration. All bombing equipment was removed, additional fuselage fuel tanks and a reel and hose refueling kit were added. Unlike the earlier tanker-package, that was removable in several hours, the KA-3B changes were fixed and those Whales served exclusively as tankers.

More than 5,000 gallons of usable fuel was carried and these tankers were welcome sights for pilots coming off strikes who were low on fuel or in danger from battle-damage. The tanker version of the Skywarrior was crewed by three. Other than the refueling fairing installation on the bottom of the fuselage located aft of the bomb bay, there was little external difference in the attack bomber and the tanker versions. KA-3Bs were operated as late as December of 1990 when the last one, serving with VAQ-34, was retired and flown to NAS Pensacola where it is now on display at the Naval Aviation Museum.

(Right) An A-3B (BuNo 144628) of VAQ-130 simulated aerial refueling with a RA-5C and F-4J Phantom (BuNo 153071) during an airshow at NATC Patuxent River, Maryland on 25 August 1973. The low-level pass was quite a crowd pleaser. (Jim Sullivan)

Detachment 4 of VAH-4 experimented with a Forest Green camouflage over Insignia White undersurfaces for a brief time during one of its Vietnam cruises. This Skywarrior tanker was returning to USS KITTY HAWK in the South China Sea during 1966. (U.S. Navy)

A KA-3B (BuNo 144627) of VAH-4 refuels an A-4C (BuNo 147798) Skyhawk of VA-113. Heavily loaded with ordnance, attack aircraft often departed the carrier with minimum fuel and once airborne they hooked up with a tanker, refueled and headed for the target. Both jets were from Carrier Air Wing Eleven aboard the USS KITTY HAWK during 1967. (Lionel Paul)

This KA-3B (BuNo 147655) of VAQ-308 carried a "Whale" marking on top of the vertical tail. It was refueling an A-4F (BuNo 154992) of VMA-134 as a F-4N from VF-301 waited its turn during May of 1978. All three aircraft flew with the Naval Reserves. The Skywarrior carried a stylized "ND" modex and a large Roman numeral II on the rear of the fuselage to make the tanker easy to identify. (Bruce Trombecky)

A KA-3B (BuNo 144627) of VAH-4 refuels a camouflaged RA-5C (BuNo 150834) of RVAH-13 high over the South China Sea off Vietnam. The Vigilante briefly wore this paint scheme while the Navy was evaluating the benefits of camouflage to cut down combat losses. Both aircraft flew from the USS KITTY HAWK (CVA-63). (Lionel Paul)

This KA-3B (BuNo 147655) of VAH-208, flying over the California coast during March of 1985, was attached to Carrier Reserve Air Wing Twenty. Skywarrior tankers carried more than 5,000 gallons of useable aviation fuel and were welcome sights to aircraft in urgent need of fuel. (USN via Peter Mersky)

This A-3B (BuNo 142635) of VAH-2 carried a Red lightning bolt on the vertical tail, while at NAS Alameda, California during November of 1965. The aircraft was attached to Carrier Air Group Fourteen aboard the USS RANGER. A short time later, Heavy Two departed on its second WESTPAC (Western Pacific) cruise. (Clay Jansson)

Wing Leading Edge Slats

A3D-1/A-3A

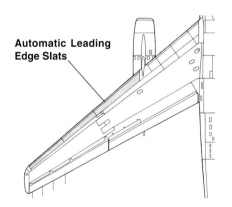

Automatic Leading Edge Slats

A3D-2/A-3B All Variants

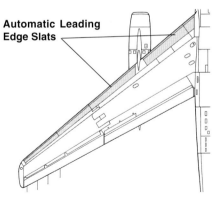

Automatic Leading Edge Slats

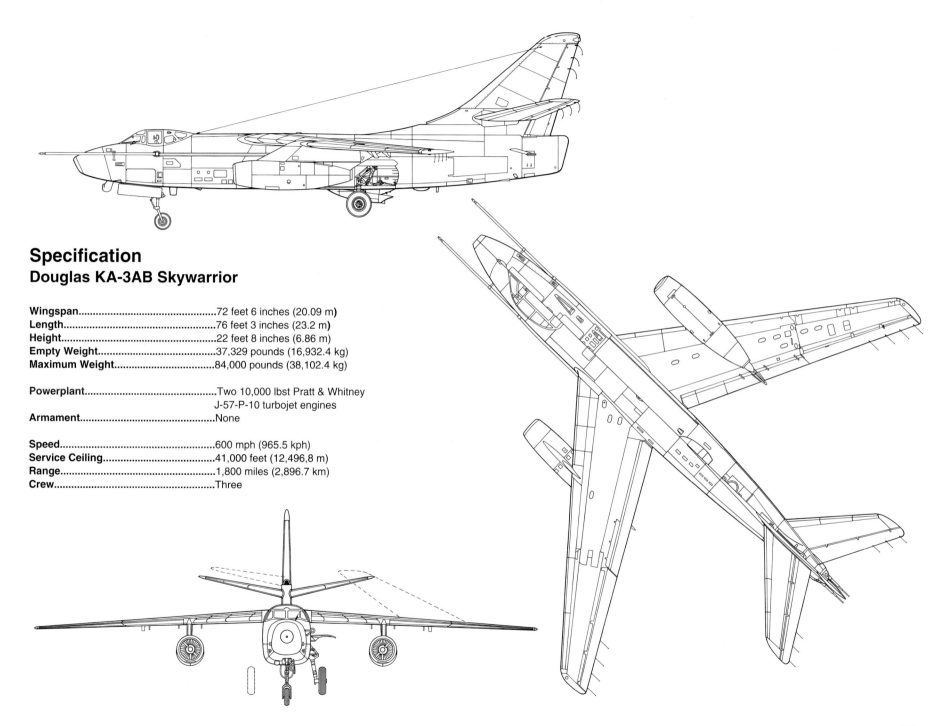

Specification
Douglas KA-3AB Skywarrior

Wingspan...72 feet 6 inches (20.09 m)
Length...76 feet 3 inches (23.2 m)
Height...22 feet 8 inches (6.86 m)
Empty Weight..37,329 pounds (16,932.4 kg)
Maximum Weight..................................84,000 pounds (38,102.4 kg)

Powerplant...Two 10,000 lbst Pratt & Whitney
                                                                J-57-P-10 turbojet engines
Armament...None

Speed...600 mph (965.5 kph)
Service Ceiling......................................41,000 feet (12,496,8 m)
Range...1,800 miles (2,896.7 km)
Crew...Three

Marked with the Red Russian star on their vertical fins, a pair of Skywarriors of VAQ-34 conduct an aerial refueling exercise (a KA-3B (#20) refuel an ERA-3B [BuNo144846]) as part of an aggressor exercise where the Skywarriors were utilized to simulate Soviet bombers making attacks on ships off Point Mugu, California during 1985. (USN via Steve Halsted)

This KA-3B (BuNo 142649) of VAH-10 was assigned to USS RANGER when not ashore at NAS North Island, California. The bomb bay doors on the Skywarrior tanker could only be opened while the Whale was on the ground. The stylized Viking sword was displayed on both sides of the fuselage. (Clay Jansson)

A KA-3B (BuNo 138966) of VAQ-133 on the flight deck of USS KITTY HAWK pierside at NAS North Island, California on 3 October 1970. The squadron was attached to Carrier Air Wing Eleven. The squadron modex and aircraft number were carried on the underside of the port wing and the trim on the fin was in Red. (Clay Jansson)

Tanker Four, a KA-3B (BuNo 142662) of VAQ-308, begins its letdown over the California countryside during 1978, while enroute to its home base at NAS Alameda, California. The national insignia was carried well to the rear on the fuselage side, followed by the large Roman numeral IV. This marking was carried to make the tanker highly visible. (USN via Peter Mersky)

(Right) A KA-3B (BuNo 142649) of VAQ-132 on the transit ramp at Udorn, Thailand during October of 1970. The aircraft carried the unit's Scorpion marking on the fuselage side just behind the cockpit. The Skywarrior was attached to Carrier Air Wing Nine and flew from the USS AMERICA. (Don Jay)

A KA-3B (BuNo 147655) of VAQ-208 banks away, revealing the external tanker installation just to the rear of of the bomb bay. (USN via Peter Mersky)

This KA-3B (BuNo 142406) of VAQ-133 was a veteran of the Vietnam war. After serving the Navy for some fourteen years, it was placed in storage at Davis Monthan AFB during August of 1970. (USN via Peter Mersky)

An EKA-3B (BuNo 142662) of VAW-13, Det. 19 was attached to Carrier Air Wing Twenty-One aboard the USS HANCOCK during 1968. This dual role ECM/tanker Skywarrior flew missions during Vietnam. The aircraft carried twin Red lightning bolts on the fuselage and a Red rudder. (U.S. Navy)

EKA-3B

The EKA-3B version was a dual-purpose modification allowing the Skywarrior to serve both as a tanker and a ECM aircraft. This version was utilized during the war in Vietnam and flew from carriers and land bases. Conversions to the EKA-3B configuration were handled by NARF Alameda who completed the modifications of thirty-nine airframes from A-3B and KA-3B Skywarriors. Externally, the EKA-3B was easily identifiable by the four large teardrop-shaped fuselage blisters that housed much of the ECM equipment and the ventral "canoe" located on the bottom of the fuselage. Although the EKA-3B had a dual-mission assignment it retained a crew of only three.

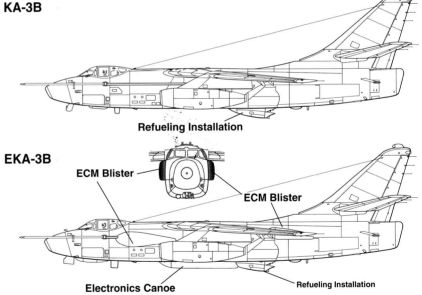

KA-3B

Refueling Installation

EKA-3B

ECM Blister

ECM Blister

Electronics Canoe

Refueling Installation

A Black Ravens EKA-3B (BuNo 142632) on the ramp at NAS Whidbey Island, Washington during 1969. Skywarriors of VAQ-135 carried the "TR" modex on the fin. The large fuselage blisters housed ECM equipment and were unique to the EKA-3B. (Pete Bowers)

This EKA-3B (BuNo 144628) of VAH-10 at NAS Whidbey Island, on 28 May 1970 carried a small Viking sword on the forward port ECM blister. (Doug Olson via Clay Jansson)

This Skywarrior retained the Viking sword and tail trim markings carried by VAH-10 before it was redesignated as VAQ-129. The EKA-3B (BuNo 142650) was flying over the Gulf of Tonkin enroute to USS HANCOCK on 18 March 1971. This Whale was operating with Carrier Air Wing Twenty-One. (USN via Peter Mersky)

An EKA-3B (BuNo 142646) of VAQ-130, Det. 4 refuels a F-4J (BuNo 148356) Phantom II of VF-21 high over the South China Sea during March of 1973. Both aircraft were flying from the USS RANGER and assigned to Carrier Air Wing Two. This Skywarrior was modified from an A-3B by NARF Alameda and served the Fleet for twenty-one years. (Jan Jacobs)

This EKA-3B (BuNo 142659) of VAW-13, on the ramp at its home port of NAS Alameda, California on 28 December 1967. Because of the location of the aft ECM blister, the national insignia was positioned far aft on the fuselage. This ECM/tanker Skywarrior served aboard the USS BON HOMME RICHARD. (Clay Jansson)

Spotted on the deck edge elevator of USS JOHN F. KENNEDY on 1 August 1970, this EKA-3B (BuNo 142252) of VAQ-131 carried five Black stripes on the aft fuselage to make Tanker Five easily identifiable. This Whale was attached to Carrier Air Group One. (Tom Cuddy II via Lionel Paul)

This EKA-3B (142403) of VAQ-131 had just returned to NAS Alameda, California on 13 September 1969 after seeing action in Vietnam as part of Carrier Air Wing Eleven aboard USS KITTY HAWK. The Lancers squadron emblem was displayed forward on the ECM blister beneath the cockpit. The port engine nacelle lower access panels were partially open. (Clay Jansson)

Operating off Vietnam in the South China sea during a WESTPAC cruise, an EKA-3B from VAQ-130, Det. 4 prepares to launch from USS ENTERPRISE during July of 1971. These Skywarriors had a dual mission, since they were capable not only of aerial refueling but also performed ECM duties. (Bob Lawson/The HOOK via Bill Brabant)

(Right) An EKA-3B (BuNo 142659) of VAQ-129 heads for the duty runway as it prepares to depart NAS Atsugi, Japan during 1970. The full span cambered leading edge slats were extended. This Whale was from the USS HANCOCK. (Hideki Nagakubo)

An EKA-3B (BuNo 142255) of VAH-130 on the ramp at its home station, NAS Whidbey Island, Washington during 1967. The fairing on the nosewheel door housed an ECM antenna. (USN via Thomas Gates)

This EKA-3B (BuNo 142634) of VAQ-130, Det. 4 flew with Carrier Air Wing Fourteen off the USS ENTERPRISE in June of 1971. This Skywarrior was later lost in an operational accident during January of 1973 off the coast of Vietnam. (Bob Lawson/The HOOK via Bill Brabant)

Carrying the 'AH' modex of Carrier Air Wing Sixteen, this EKA-3B (BuNo 142237) of VAQ-130 was parked on the ramp at Mather AFB, California on 5 December 1970. (Don Spering/A.I.R.)

37

This A3D-2T (BuNo 144867) of VAH-123 at NAS Whidbey Island, Washington on 18 April 1962, was used to train A-3 crews in the use of airborne radar and navigational equipment. (Doug Olson via Clay Jansson)

A3D-2T/TA-3B

Douglas produced twelve A3D-2T/TA-3B Skywarriors (BuNo 144856-144867), the first of which flew on 29 August 59. This version was a navigation and tactical crew training model and had provisions for the pilot, an instructor and six students. The spacious fuselage was pressurized and ideal for the installation of radar/navigational training equipment. Easily identifiable from other versions, the A3D-2T/TA-3B had square windows installed in the forward fuselage, three on the starboard and four on the port side. Some of these trainers were later modified to accommodate passengers and were used as VIP transports. In that configuration,

seats were added along with a small galley and lavatory. With those items removed, the Skywarrior could also operate as a jet COD or cargo aircraft.

A TA-3B (BuNo 144866) of VAQ-130 on the ramp at NAS Lemoore, California on 10 October 1971 was one of twelve "trainers" produced by Douglas Aircraft. This version of the Skywarrior carried a crew of eight in the pressurized fuselage. (Clay Jansson)

A TA-3B (BuNo 144861) of RVAH-3 on the ramp at NAS Sanford, Florida on 26 May 1967 carried Red bands on the fin and rudder. One of the crew was looking out of the open cockpit escape hatch. (Clay Jansson)

This TA-3B (BuNo 144865) of VR-1 on the ramp at MCAS Yuma on 17 March 1973, carried an American Flag marking on the vertical fin above the JK modex. This Skywarrior was being used as a VIP transport. (Clay Jansson)

This sharkmouthed TA-3B of VAQ-33 at NAS Key West, Florida during April of 1991 was nearing the end of its military career. The last active Skywarrior was retired from active service on 27 September 1991. (Don Spering/A.I.R.)

This VA-3B (BuNo 142672) was one of five converted from A3D-2Qs to the VIP transport role. This Skywarrior was based at NAF Washington DC and was used by the CNO (Chief of Naval Operations) as his personal transport. (Clay Jansson)

This TA-3B (BuNo 144862) on the transit ramp at NAS Oceana on 28 April 1979 was used by VAQ-33 Firebirds for training East Coast Skywarrior crews and was based at NAS Norfolk, Virginia. (Jim Sullivan)

This TA-3B (BuNo 144859) of RVAH-3 was visiting Kelly Air Force Base, Texas on 17 January 1976. This was the fourth TA-3B built. (Dr. Carlton Eddy)

With its landing gear almost fully retracted, this VA-3B (BuNo 144857) thundered out of NAF Washington, DC on 24 April 1973. This Skywarrior was assigned to the Department of the Navy and was used to transport VIPs. (Jim Sullivan)

An EA-3B (BuNo 146449) of VQ-I displayed "the rapid-rabbit" Playboy bunny insignia on its vertical fin during July of 1974. The aircraft was on final approach for landing at NAF Atsugi, Japan. This Skywarrior was equipped with an array of three blade antennas low on the forward fuselage side and the speed brakes were extended. (Hideki Nagakubo)

A3D-2Q/EA-3B

Douglas manufactured twenty-four A3D-2Q/EA-3B Skywarriors, with the first flight taking place on 10 December 1958. The first Fleet deliveries of this ECM/reconnaissance version of the Whale were to VQ-1 in November of 1959. In addition to the standard flight crew of three, the A3D-2Q variant had provisions for four operators for the ECM missions. Operating from carriers or land bases, the primary mission of the A3D-2Q/EA-3B was to provide threat warnings of SAM site activity, while locating the origin of their emitters. Another mission was the collection of additional electronic signals and transmissions of interest to Fleet intelligence.

To provide for ease of entry or emergency exit, the EA-3B was fitted with a crew hatch on the starboard side of the fuselage near the wing leading edge. The seven man crew operated in an air-conditioned, pressurized environment which allowed them to perform their duties at any altitude without the cumbersome oxygen mask. This long range version of the Skywarrior was powered by two P&W J-57 turbojets, had a top speed of 550 knots and had an operating range of more than 2,500 miles. As the ECM version of the Intruder became available, the EA-3Bs were phased out of service.

(Above and Below) EA-3B's of VQ-1 line the ramp at their home station, NAF Atsugi, Japan during 1971. These Skywarriors saw extensive use during the Vietnam war, flying from both carriers and land bases. (Clay Jansson Collection)

An EA-3B of VQ-1 heads toward the deck edge elevator after trapping aboard the USS RANGER during November of 1974. This version of the Whale was used for ECM/reconnaissance missions and carried a crew of seven. (Bruce Trombecky)

Flown by LCDR Roy New, this EA-3B of VQ-2 lifted off the runway and retracted its landing gear almost immediately. This version of the Skywarrior had a fuselage entry/escape hatch to accommodate the four ECM operators. (USN via Fred Carment)

This EA-3B (BuNo 146455) of VQ-2 on the ramp at NAS Alameda, California on 12 June 1982 carried the modex "JQ" and a stylized "Bat" design on the vertical fin. This Skywarrior was in service for more than twenty-five years. (Tom Chee via Don Spering/A.I.R. Collection)

Safely down from a mission over Vietnam, this EA-3B of VQ-I snagged the #1 wire aboard the USS RANGER while the ship was operating in the Tonkin Gulf in April of 1973. (Jan Jacobs)

41

Operating from Da Nang Air Base in South Vietnam, an EA-3B of VQ-1 returns from a mission during 1966. The Skywarrior, side number 14, moved down the taxiway to the ramp where it would be serviced and await its next flight. (Clay Jansson Collection)

An EA-3B takes on fuel during aerial refueling from an Air Force KC-135 tanker. This Skywarrior flew with VAQ-33, a Tactical Electronic Warfare Squadron in 1979. (LT Pete Griffiths via Steve Halsted)

Starting its service career in October of 1959, this EA-3B (BuNo 142671) of VQ-1 recovered aboard USS CONSTELLATION on 18 April 1985 some twenty-five years later . This Skywarrior served the Navy for over twenty-six years and had stenciling on the aft fuselage which read "Handle With Care, On Loan From The Smithsonian Institution." (Rick Morgan via Bruce Trombecky)

Having recovered safely aboard the USS KITTY HAWK during operations in the South China Sea in 1973, this EA-3B, side number 7, of VQ-1 folded its wings and headed for the deck edge elevator. (Lionel Paul)

When the VQ-1 detachment first reported aboard USS KITTY HAWK, they had a plain fin with just the modex PR on it. A young IS1 (Intelligence Specialist First) attached to the ship's intellignece center designed the tail design for the squadron for a fee of $10. That IS1 is now the editor for squadron/signal publications. (Nicholas J. Waters III)

(Right) An EA-3B (BuNo 146452) of VQ-1 on the flight line at NAS Agana, Guam on 18 April 1985. This ECM Skywarrior had a small Whale design on its nose forward of the "003" side number. (Bruce Trombecky)

Crew Entry/Exit Door

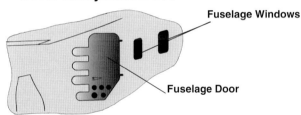

Fuselage Windows

Fuselage Door

Spotted with F-4B Phantoms of VF-114 and VF-213, an EA-3B of VQ-1 awaits its next mission aboard USS KITTY HAWK while the ship was operating in the Tonkin Gulf off the coast of Vietnam in 1972. This particular deployment for the KITTY HAWK lasted some nine and a half months. (Lionel Paul)

This EA-3B (BuNo 144849) of VAQ-34 sports the Red Russian star on its vertical fin. The Skywarrior was from the West coast and was visiting NAF Washington, DC in May of 1990. The aircraft was used to simulate enemy aircraft conducting attacks on the Fleet. (Charles E. Taylor)

This EA-3B of VQ-2 on the ramp at NAS North Island, California during 1973 carried the Spanish "Spook" design on its vertical fin. (Bob Lawson/The HOOK)

43

This A3D-2P (BuNo 144847) of VCP-63 on the ramp at NAS Miramar, California on 26 January 1960, was one of thirty photo reconnaissance Skywarriors built by Douglas. This Whale could carry up to twelve cameras. (Clay Jansson)

A3D-2P/RA-3B

Douglas manufactured thirty of the photo-reconnaissance A3D-2P/RA-3B Skywarriors. First flown on 22 July 1958, this long-range jet photographic aircraft greatly expanded the eyes of the Fleet. Crewed by four, the RA-3B carried up to twelve cameras for vertical and oblique photography. Externally, the RA-3B could be easily recognized by the camera ports and fairings located low on both sides of the fuselage forward of the bomb bay. Serving with only three squadrons (VAP-61, VAP-62 and VCP-63), these Skywarriors could fly day or night missions. For night photography the RA-3B carried flash bombs or flash cartridges. While some early production photo Skywarriors initially carried the tail-mounted twin 20MM cannon installation, it was soon deleted in favor of the ECM type tail fairing. After their service in the reconnaissance role was completed, three airframes were modified to NRA-3Bs for use in missile system development work and others were reconfigured as ERA-3Bs for Fleet electronic warfare support.

Camera Ports

RA-3B

Forward Oblique Camera   Side Oblique Cameras

Serving with VAP-61, this A3D-2P (BuNo 144844) carried the Black modex "SS" on its vertical fin. The photo-recon Skywarrior carried a crew of four and was visiting NAF Washington, DC on 26 September 1961. (USN via Peter Mersky)

This VCP-63 Skywarrior was an A3D-2P (BuNo 144842). PP-930 taxies by palm trees at NAS Agana, Guam during June of 1962 as a crew member looks out the cockpit escape hatch. (USN via Peter Mersky)

The main instrument panel of a RA-3B. The camera control section was located just to the right of the center console. (Douglas via Harry Gann)

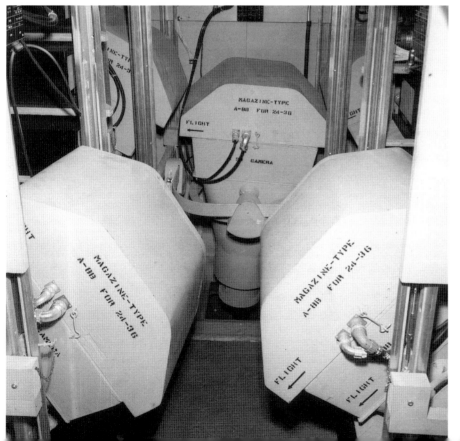

Turning onto a short final, this RA-3B (BuNo 144833) from the Naval Air Test Center at Patuxent River was landing at the Pacific MIssile Test Center at Pt. Mugu, California during November of 1979. (Peter Bergagnini via Bruce Trombecky)

This RA-3B (BuNo 144833) wore the markings of the Naval Air Development Center high on its vertical fin. The aircraft was visiting NAS Willow Grove, PA during 1975. (Bob Esposito)

(Left) A3D-2P camera installation in the forward fuselage looking to the rear from the cockpit. (Douglas via Harry Gann)

This RA-3B (BuNo 144843) was moments away from landing at NAF Atsugi, Japan during 1973. This Skywarrior later flew "research" missions with the U.S. Army. (Hideki Nagakubo)

45

(Above) This RA-3B (BuNo 144840) Skywarrior of VAP-61 carried an unusual Gray and Blue camouflage for missions over North Vietnam. The aircraft was at NAS North Island, California on 26 November 1968. This Whale was modified in 1974 to become a NRA-3B and worked with missile systems and special programs. (Clay Jansson)

(Left) A RA-3B, side number 8 of VAP-62, breaks right, revealing the underside camera ports. Photo Skywarriors were capable of day or night photography. Heavy Photographic Squadron Two was stationed at NAS Jacksonville, Florida during October of 1964. (USN via Steve Halsted)

(Below) This RA-3B (BuNo 144843), on the ramp at NAS Alameda, California on 7 November 1981, was loaned to the Army and participated in missile test programs. Later, it was bailed (loaned) to Raytheon for their use in testing various electronic systems. (Tom Chee via Bruce Trombecky)

46

An ERA-3B (BuNo 146446) of VAQ-33 retracts its landing gear at very low level as it departed NAS Oceana, Virginia on 23 March 1990. This East coast Skywarrior was attached to the Fleet Electronic Warfare Support Group (FEWSG) and flew as an electronic aggressor during fleet exercises. (Bruce Trombecky)

A pair of ERA-3Bs (BuNos 146446 and 146447) of VAQ-33 Firebirds fly high over the Pacific off the California coast during May of 1983. Both Skywarriors were equipped with a chaff-dispensing installation in the elongated tail section. The flight originated at NAS Miramar, California. (Bruce Trombecky)

(Right) This ERA-3B (BuNo 144838) of VAQ-34 was departing the NMTC at Point Mugu, California on 21 November 1988. VAQ-34 was a West coast squadron attached to the Fleet Electronis Warfare Support Group (FEWSG). The black modex "GD" was decorated with two Red lightning bolts on the vertical tail. (Bruce Trombecky)

The forward instrument panel of an ERA-3B (BuNo 144846). This Skywarrior was assigned to VAQ-34 and was modified from a RA-3B by NARF Alameda, California during 1982. (Bruce Trombecky)

ERA-3B

A total of ten RA-3B Skywarriors were modified by NARF Alameda to the ERA-3B configuration and served exclusively with two squadrons, VAQ-33 and VAQ-34. These Whales were used for long-range reconnaissance and electronic surveillance and communications jamming. Equipped with chaff dispensers located in the tail, these Skywarriors were most effective in confusing enemy radar and superb in locating unfriendly emitters and targeting them for destruction. Because of their weight, ERA-3Bs operated only from land bases. With underwing pylons for ECM pods and RAT (Ram Air Turbine) installations on each side of the fuselage, as well as the ventral fuselage mounted "canoe", the ERA-3B was easily identifiable. This version of the Skywarrior carried the normal flight crew of three plus two ECM evaluators.

This ERA-3B (BuNo 144827) of VAQ-33 was lined up for final approach at NAS Oceana, Virginia, on 11 May 1978. The Skywarrior carried an ECM pod on its underwing pylon outboard of the engine nacelle. (Jim Sullivan)

(Left) This ERA-3B (BuNo 144841) of VAQ-34 carried a Red Russian star on its vertical tail and the number 12 in Russian style lettering on the nose. This "electric aggressor" Skywarrior was at the PMTC at Point Mugu, California, on 21 November 1987. (Bruce Trombecky)

An ERA-3B (BuNo 144827) of VAQ-33 on the flight line at NAS Miramar, California during October of 1983. This Skywarrior carried a yellow "Pacman" design on the flat nose radome. The RAT (Ram Air Turbine) installation was low on the fuselage beneath the circular window. (Bruce Trombecky)

An ERA-3B (BuNo 144841) of VAQ-34 in flight over the Pacific off the California coast during October of 1983. This Skywarrior had the earlier dove-tail faring installation, but has chaff dispensers on the fuselage sides. GD-212 was flying from NAS Miramar, California. (Bruce Trombecky)

This ERA-3B (BuNo 144832) of VAQ-33 carries a low-vis overall Gray paint scheme. This version of the Whale represented the ultimate modification of the 1959 vintage airframe. Its twenty-four foot drag chute billowing out behind it, this Skywarrior was one of the last few still flying in April of 1991 and was soon retired from service. (Don Spering/A.I.R.)

(Right) Parked on the flight line at NAS Oceana, Virginia on 12 May 1977, this ERA-3B (BuNo 146447) had the forward entry hatch left open. The open hatch door on the rear fuselage was a small baggage compartment. An ECM pod was carried on the underwing pylon. (Jim Sullivan)

Its military career completed, this ERA-3B (BuNo 146446) carried the civil code N161TB and was flown, along with several others, by Thunderbird Aviation collecting research data. The aircraft was based at Deer Valley Airport, Phoenix, AZ on 20 March 1992. (Joe Handelman, DDS)

This NRA-3B (BuNo 144825) on the ramp at NAF Washington, DC on 6 November 1982, was a one-of-a-kind modification. This large nose radome was installed by Grumman for use in testing missile systems. More non-standard modifications were installed on the aft end of the fuselage. (Don Linn)

49

U.S. NAVY JETS
FROM
squadron/signal publications

1103

1105

1120

1136

1140